BEDTIME LULLABY

This book belongs to:

. . . .

Twinkle Twinkle, Little Star

Twinkle twinkle, little star,
How I wonder what you are.
Up above the world so high,
Like a diamond in the sky.
Twinkle twinkle, little star,
How I wonder what you are.

Rock-a-bye Baby

Rock-a-bye baby, in the treetop.
When the wind blows, the cradle will rock,
When the bough breaks, the cradle will fall,
Down will come baby, cradle and all.

Come to the Window

Come to the window,
My baby, with me,
And look at the stars
That shine on the sea.
There are two little stars
That play bo-peep,
With two little fish
Far down in the deep;
And two little frogs
Cry, "Neap, neap, neap";
I see a dear baby
That should be asleep.

Where Should a Baby Rest?

Where should a baby rest?
Where but on its mother's arm.
Where can a baby lie
Half so safe from every harm?
Lulla, lulla, lullaby,
Softly sleep my baby.
Lulla, lulla, lullaby,
Soft, soft my baby.

Nestle there, my lovely one,
Press to mine thy velvet cheek.
Sweetly coo, and smile, and look,
All the love thou canst not speak.
Lulla, lulla, lullaby,
Softly sleep my baby.
Lulla, lulla, lullaby,
Soft, soft my baby.

Lavender's Blue

Lavender's blue, dilly, dilly,
Lavender's green;
When you are King, dilly, dilly,
I shall be Queen.

Call up your friends, dilly, dilly,
Set them to work;
Some to the plow, dilly, dilly,
Some to the fork.

Some to make hay, dilly, dilly,
Some to thresh corn;
While you and I, dilly, dilly,
Keep ourselves warm.

Lavender's blue, dilly, dilly,
Lavender's green;
When I am King, dilly, dilly,
You shall be Queen.

Hush Little Baby

Hush little baby, don't say a word,
Papa's gonna buy you a mockingbird.
If that mockingbird don't sing,
Papa's gonna buy you a diamond ring.

If that diamond ring turns to brass,
Papa's gonna buy you a looking glass.
If that looking glass gets broke,
Papa's gonna buy you a billy goat.

If that billy goat won't pull,

Papa's gonna buy you a cart and bull.

If that cart and bull turn over,

Papa's gonna buy you a dog named Rover.

If that dog named Rover won't bark,

Papa's gonna buy you a horse and cart.

If that horse and cart fall down,

You'll be the sweetest little baby in town.

Star Light, Star Bright

Star light, star bright,

First star I see tonight.

I wish I may, I wish I might,

Have the wish I wish tonight.

Bye, Baby Bunting

Bye, baby bunting,

Daddy's gone a-hunting,

A rosy wisp of cloud to win

To wrap the baby bunting in.

Bye, baby bunting.

Brahms' Lullaby

Lullaby and good night,
In the sky stars are bright.
'Round your head flowers gay
Scent your slumber till day.

Close your eyes now and rest,
May these hours be blessed.
Go to sleep now and rest
May your slumber be blessed.

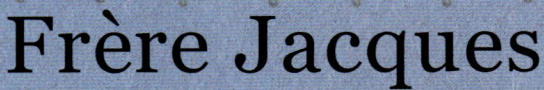

Frère Jacques

Frère Jacques, Frère Jacques,

Dormez-vous? Dormez-vous?

Sonnez les matines,

Sonnez les matines,

Din, din, don. Din, din, don.

Are you sleeping, are you sleeping?

Brother John? Brother John?

Morning bells are ringing,

Morning bells are ringing,

Ding, ding, dong. Ding, ding, dong.

The Man in the Moon

The man in the Moon
Looked out of the Moon
And this is what he said:
"'Tis time for all children on the Earth
To think about getting to bed."

Matthew, Mark, Luke and John

Matthew, Mark, Luke and John,

Bless the bed that I lie on.

Four corners to my bed,

Four angels 'round my head.

One to watch and one to pray

And two to bear my soul away.

Rocking Carol

Little baby, sweetly sleep, do not stir,
We will lend a coat of fur.

We will rock you, rock you, rock you,
We will rock you, rock you, rock you.

See the fur to keep you warm,
Gently round your tiny form.

Precious little baby, sleep, sweetly sleep,
Sleep in comfort, slumber deep.

We will rock you, rock you, rock you,
We will rock you, rock you, rock you.

Little baby, do not cry,
We will sing a lullaby.

Sleep, Baby, Sleep

Sleep, baby, sleep,
Your father guards the sheep.
Your mother shakes the dreamland tree
And from it fall sweet dreams for thee.
Sleep, baby, sleep.

Sleep, baby, sleep,
Our cottage vale is deep.
The little lamb is on the green,
With snowy fleece so soft and clean.
Sleep, baby, sleep.

Sleep, baby, sleep,
Down where the woodbines creep.
Be always like the lamb so mild,
A kind, and sweet, and gentle child.
Sleep, baby, sleep.

Winkum, Winkum

Winkum, winkum, shut your eyes
While I sing sweet lullabies;
For the dews are falling soft,
Lights are flick'ring up aloft;
And the moonlight's peeping over
Yonder hilltop capped with clover.

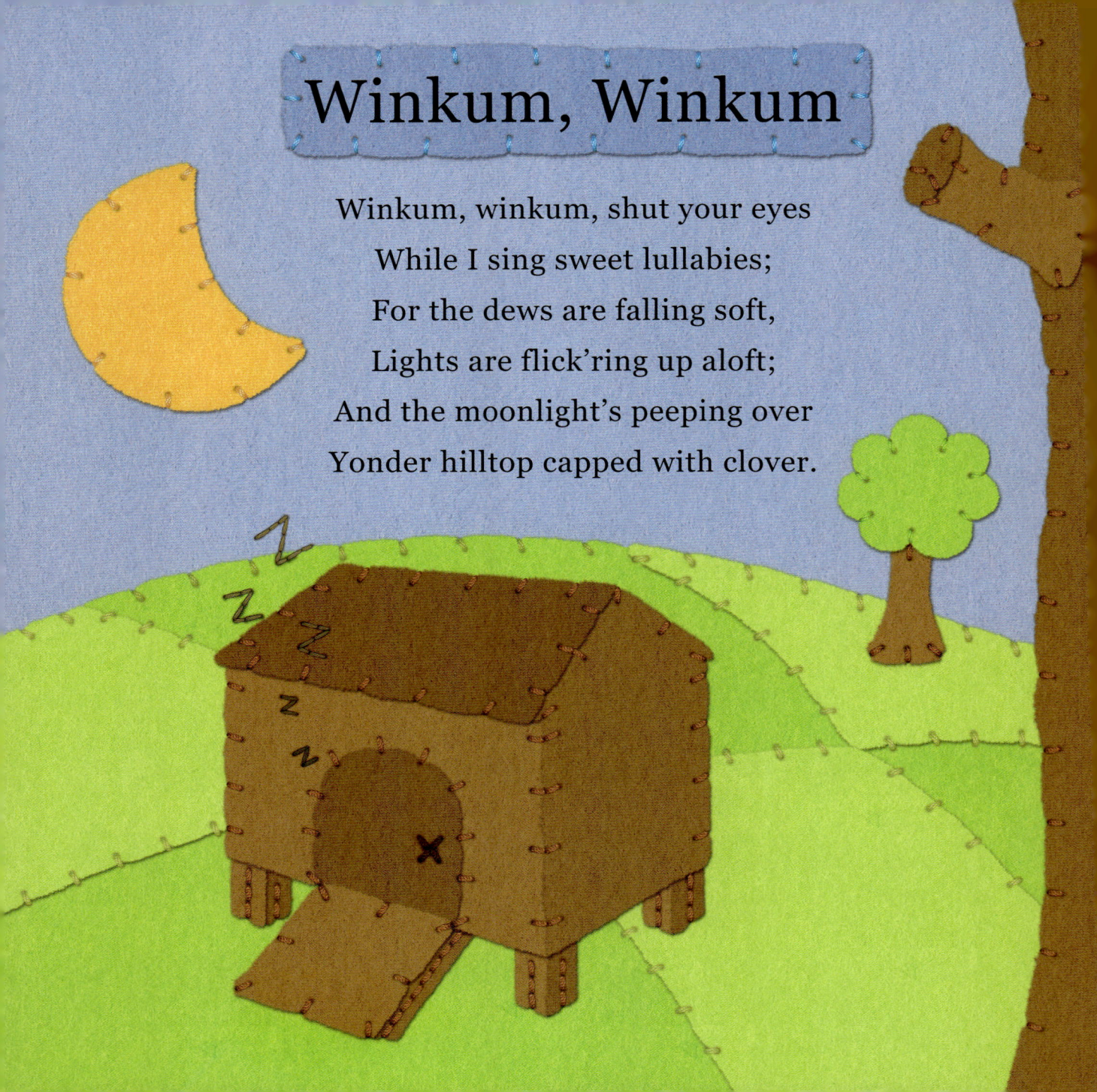

Chickens long have gone to rest,
Birds lie snug within their nest.
And my darling soon will be
Sleeping like a chickadee.
For with only half a try,
Winkum, winkum shuts her eyes.

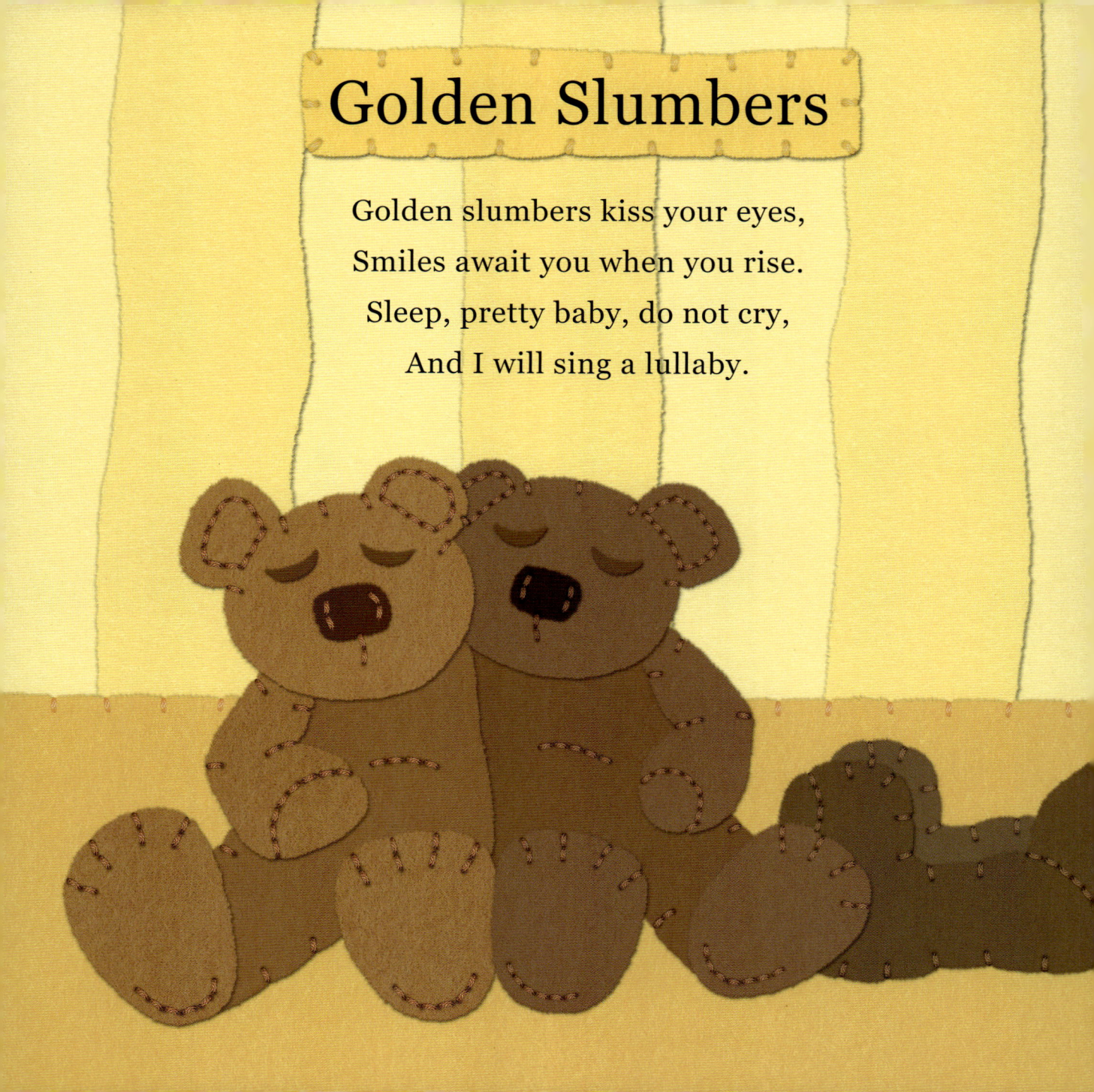

Golden Slumbers

Golden slumbers kiss your eyes,
Smiles await you when you rise.
Sleep, pretty baby, do not cry,
And I will sing a lullaby.

Care you know not, therefore sleep,
While I o'er you watch do keep.
Sleep, pretty baby, do not cry,
And I will sing a lullaby.